SCATTERED RAYS

SCATTERED RAYS

AN EMOTIONAL ASSORTMENT OF POEMS

SHIVANGI RAWAT

Woven Words Publishers OPC Pvt. Ltd.

Registered Office:

Vill: Raipur, P.O: Raipur Paschimbar,

Dist: Purba Midnapore, Pin: 721401,

West Bengal, India.

www.wovenwordspublishers.in

Email: editor@wovenwordspublishers.in

First published by Woven Words Publishers OPC Pvt. Ltd., 2018

Copyright© Shivangi Rawat, 2018

POETRY

IMPRINT: WOVEN WORDS FIRE

ISBN 13: 978-93-86897-17-6

ISBN 10: 9386897172

Price: 10$/₹120

This book is a work of fiction. All names, characters, places, addresses and incidents are fictitious and product of the author's imagination. Any resemblance with any events, locales, persons-living or dead, is purely coincidental.

The author asserts the moral right to be identified as the author of this work.

All rights reserved. This book is sold to the condition that it shall not, by way of trade or otherwise, be lent, resold, hired out, or otherwise circulated without the publisher's prior consent in any form of binding or cover other than that in which it is published and without a similar condition, including this condition, being imposed on the subsequent purchaser.

ACKNOWLEDGEMENT

I would like to express my gratitude to many people who provided support, talked things over, read, offered, comments and encouraged me to write.

Specifying names is the hardest part for me. Many times, even the nano-est bit of encouragement all you need to gear up or pump up yourself and that may arrive unexpectedly from unknown or anyone. So, if I miss your name accept my apology and forgive me and please know that your support was crucial as well and bless me all I need from my close once.

I would like to extend my thanks to first and most to almighty for showering blessing and giving an opportunity to take birth as a human being. Now to the person who is equal to almighty my father **Mr. Kamlesh Rawat**. I want to give him thanks which I generally don't do. To my grandmother Mrs. **Asharani Rawat** a cancer survivor, she is always an example for being a determined and strong, my uncle **Mr. Brajesh Rawat** and aunt **Mrs. Sangeeta Rawat**.

Special thanks to my second mom, my besti, my heart, my only sister **Mrs. Akanksha Gupta** and my Brother-in -law **Mr. Shiva Gupta**. Also, want to thank our house junior one who will proceed legacy ahead **Master Shriram Rawat** my brother.

Especial thanks to **Mrs. Nita Samantaray** mam for always being with me, **Mosiur Rehman** sir for helping me in Publishing and keeping me in the board of authors of Woven Words Publishers.

Humble thanks to all my friends and of course online friend, readers, writers and reviewers. Resting my pen, but I would like to thank last whoever have helped me in this long journey from being ordinary to extraordinary as now I'm an Author.

Shivangi Rawat

SAGA OF LOVE

Inside my core,

Something killed me before

No more tears left to fall,

No more moments to recall.

All day searching for my phone book,

Waiting for his first look.

With umpteen queries in my mind,

finding someone same as me to kind.

Fading his betrayal memories,

coming out of drenched gloomy thoughts.

Someone came with another light,

 making my world so bright.

Pulling me out and changing my soul,

Healing my cracks of heart and holes.

But, I'm afraid of history now that is a mystery.

Oh! He is a gem

Made me smile and the saga of love continued to sail.

MY HOME

In dark and unknown

I thought not to wander

into the forest that is

so intense and grown.

I was all alone

With the soul of

My beloved, to whom

I meet there and then I know

I have nothing left to fear.

I walk down, holding my beloved hand tight,

He illuminates the way and creates a path.

That dark night became a bright day of light

 with love and faith.

Broken from the deep slumber,

I found me under the quilt.

I was never alone; the truth was revealed.

It was his chest and I call it my home.

I AM

I am worthy

Yes, I am worthy of praise,

I am worthy of peace,

I am worthy of love,

I am worthy of respect,

I am worthy of joy,

I am worthy of happiness.

Throughout all of the cosmos

and

 out of millions of folks

in this world, I chose to love MYSELF.

ICELAND of TRUST

Through my blurry faded vision

With a heart so pure

I searched you to come back

Sail our ship not to shore

But too far from this chaotic world

With a hope to ignite the flame of Love again

Respire together in the peace with fireflies

Near the ICELAND of TRUST.

YOU ARE MY WORDS

As you are gone far

I have written you on my ink

I read you in my verses

But I don't forget you in my pages.

I miss you each and every second

I speak of you again and again

Try to connect by telepathy

But I fail.

I guard you in my characters of fiction

I made you my imaginations.

We have parted but I have

Shrouded you in my art

Time will age but my love will not.

I have made you my poems and haikus

Every time I miss you

I write and

So, you are my WORDs

YOU WILL ALWAYS FIND ME NEAR

I am so humble

That you are here

Be my shadow

To which I don't fear

Be the reason for smile

Which I wear.

I don't want to be a burden

For which you regret or

Have to bear.

Take a time to analyze

There is no hurry nor to be so worry

I will never go away

You will always find me near.

DEPRESSION

Thoughts make me think of death

There is a pinch of darkness which blanks my mind

Is this a depression going through my head?

I feel I want to go to hell or I am

Already in a land that is not less than hell.

I am in a place full of sadness

A place full of despair.

I have nothing to live for

I have no past no future

So, I think I shall end it, end

This life at last.

Passing through graveyard, seeing graves

The feeling of lying in box

Six feet under if not more

How I would like to go down and explore

And once I am buried I will be locked.

Pondering, after my last breath

I will be a shadow in between to millions of graves.

After this end of melancholy life

I will wait, another one to take

With a new moon and sun

Will embrace my life again.

DEMONS OF MY MIND

I stood on Cambridge

In silence with fear

Demons of darkness compelled

And drove me here.

Demons of dark cut my heart

Pull out from my chest

Making me believe

That they know me best.

Demons of dark were always there

Sometimes near or sometimes far

Waiting in background

Mocking from behind.

They were destructive

Knocking down the life I knew

I hated everything about them

And they made me hate myself too.

I can't see them

They are far from fairy tales,

They are habituated in my mind

With their evilness.

So, on the Cambridge

I stood to end the fight

But I realized I, not a coward.

With a peace, I took a step back

My thoughts made me stop and

 I thought to fight with demons

One more night.

SHE FOUND HER

She woke up from the deep slumber

And found it was a witty nightmare

In which she found you

Creasing her with love.

She was broken chord,

Floating, untethered

In a discordant symphony

Until she remembered

All that she was,

And all that she worth.

Now she lives in harmony

Upon this earth

Finally, she found her

Place in the divine orchestra

Of eternal grace.

REGRET

you have left me alone in the street,

walking under heavy rain staring at my feet.

from my agonizing pain, salty and

the blood stain, splashing on my feet

yes, it is my tears and not the drop of rain.

I was MAD to love YOU

Why was I so stupid? To hug you

Never will be able to love again

It's because of Scars you given.

Yes, it was more than JUST, I was

In a trap of LUST, that TORTURED

Me and the reason for my BROKEN TRUST.

When my pen hits paper, stained RED

Thoughts run loose, WORD come to my mind is

REGRET!

I made a mistake, you are my biggest regret

I regret every memory, every tear,

Every cupid moments and every "I LOVE YOU"

We shared, every last word that I spend wasting on someone like you

Is a Regret.

BE REALISTIC

It's hard to define in short period of time

How "YOU" have become "MINE".

You have already conquered my heart,

You are the one who adds color to my drawing chart,

You are the one who keeps me awake,

You are the one I want to see whole in my life;

Walking besides, holding my hand tight,

Waiting for the moment; with you

So, I can live that like it has no end.

I want to say aloud; you made me go crazy and

Fill water in my rainy clouds.

Tell me the best way how could I express these deep feelings of mine,

They are hovering in the sky like a kite with thread white.

It's a DREAM broken in mid of noon nap.

YOU and ME parallel line, never can meet in this lifetime.

Am I searching, that does not EXIT?

But for sure I want YOU to be realistic.

BEAUTY MARKS

I know my scars are scary

But they don't need any mercy.

I don't want anyone to peel instead

I want someone to feel and heal.

I know these scars reveal my past,

But I want you to kiss them hard.

Make me feel whole like a

Fresh flower in a bass.

I know you are the one who could

Knit my scatted pieces together in a frame.

I want you to appreciate these scars as

BEAUTY MARKS.

LOVELAND

In our love land my love we will dance and romance

Moon will watch us as an audience.

We will take a flight to our dreams,

Under the dark radiant celestial light of night.

We will explore Jupiter and Mars,

Also, will waltz among the stars.

We will fear but together we will tear the clouds,

As heartbeats will fast and a way to loud;

We will float and swim on the white floppy foam of cloud.

Our feet will have wings and will dance to the sultry beat.

We will be in the place where no one will exist

But YOU and I above-above the sky will fly so high.

I will we safe from all harms just you hold me in your arms

we will share each other's warmth.

We will be in the place where I want to belong,

Come, my BAE see all near us playing our favorite song.

Never want to be free, hold me close I want to be in your CAPTIVE OF LOVE.

We will never apart so, dance with me SWEETHEART.

YOU ARE MY SERENDIPITY

I was hurt; you healed

I was humiliated; you magnified

I was judged; you justified

I hated myself; you loved me with flare

I lost my feel; you ignited the zeal to my lost feel

I was going through worst; you made me yours first

I was walking over gorse; you offered me bed of roses

I was sad and wanted solace; you made me smile as you have mavericked in your own style…

It is my fortune I found you in my life; maybe little late but now we are true "SOULMATES"

OH, MY LOVE

I know my love

if it's not today, then it's tomorrow for sure

don't be dishearten honey, we have 7 lives more.

In this lifetime we can't flow as we are in,

soon we have to let go this as far as the moon.

You are my wing so I flutter so high, over the sky

Oh, my love, you are the song, I only can understand and be shy.

Our love is not penurious of time,

it just need a moment to tune in love and shine

You never know the future which can be divine,

 make our 'stars' for you to be mine.

Not so soon little later time,

Oh, my love, you will be mine and together we will shine….

(Published in Rainbow of womanhood: an anthology of poems and short stories by Purlitica Publication)

I LOVE

The flare in your eyes,

The warmth of your skin,

The breath of yours on my neck

That quivers within.

The touch of your hand,

The aroma of your hair,

The mildness in your smile,

The lustiness in your eagle eyes

Your kiss on my lips,

Your body near mine,

The tickle of your touch,

The feeling inside.

The sound of your voice,

The tenderness your embrace,

The hush in your stride,

The power in your face.

The calming of your presence,

The throbbing of your heart,

The promise of tomorrow

That we will never be apart.

The beauty of you kiss and magic in your touch,

It's for all these reasons I love you most.

(Published in Rainbow of womanhood: an anthology of poems and short stories by Purlitica Publication)

LOVE

Love is like sky

it gives you a power to fly.

Love is like moon

it makes you shine.

Love is a feeling;

that helps you in healing.

Love is the essence of soul;

that can be induced in two whole.

Love is a little shy

that makes you go crazy and high.

Love is prime, its value is divine.

Love is treasure,

that can be measured.

Love is beauty hidden,

that is not at all sudden.

Love is sweet melody,

that gives you clang slowly.

Love is a spark to embark.

Love is madness;

that gives you tears of sadness and happiness.

Love is canvas,

that can be colored by feelings of two hearts.

Love is like rush,

that has its own little mas magic.

Love is sunshine,

a little like a red wine.

Love is hangover;

sometimes that last forever.

Love is not a captive cage;

it is liberal that can grow old by age.

Love is not vague;

To be specific it is transparent purest to eternity.

Love is not about infidelity or treachery;

it's all about vintage classy.

(Published in Blessed Despair – a book on love, healing, and self-revelation by Artson Publishing House)

I WANT TO BE

I want to be the one

who could heal your wounds

and scars of past.

I want to be the one

who could console

your worries of future.

I want to be the one

who could enlighten

your darkness.

I want to be the one

who could realize your

never-ending dreams.

I want to be the one

who could preserve

memories forever.

I want to be the one

who could be a smile

on your lips.

I want to be the one

who could believe

in all your miracles.

I want to be the one

who could constellation

in your imagination.

I want to be the one

who could be the warmth

in the cold of your vintage heart.

I want to be the one

who could share sore

of your storms.

I want to be the one who could be a destiny of your soul and heart.

(Published in Blessed Despair – a book on love, healing and self-revelation by Artson Publishing House)

STAY POSITIVE

Scream aloud, drag it out

don't allow NEGATIVITY to stay

and become your parasite,

its solo motive is to ruin your life,

be the emperor of your own

kick NEGATIVITY aside,

live a healthy LIFE.

It always hurts, it always stings,

Who has faced know how you feels

But, don't let yourself down

When you feel shady, foggy or gloomy

Just stay Calm.

Keep your head up, never look down

In the coming future, you will be the one

Wearing CROWN.

Nothing is permanent in this world

everything changes, what can help you

is to have patience and dwell.

Open your heart, welcome

POSITIVE thoughts

So, plebs, sit down, have rest

Positive vibes and ideas are creations BEST!

NATURE teaches us

The river can be without brothers

The stars can be without mothers,

The night can be without day

So, we have to be positive in every way.

People with good heart always stay,

Chore of life goes day by day,

Sharing dreams in a healthy always

So, we have to be positive in every way.

All above,

Our universe is fantastic we can say,

The star of night always shines there,

The moon is always brighter and fair

So, we have to be positive everywhere.

I DON'T WANT

After so long you are near me

and I am in your arms,

just like that crescent moon

I want to wrap my soul in You.

You know I am insomniac,

Sinking every night in deep thought

of you under this dark sky,

ohh your tender embrace could make me feel

relaxed and help me to get some sleep.

But before a sound sleep, I want to memorize

This moment of 'WE' to freeze

Talk me about the night, the star, the moon

Let them be the witness to our long distance

Love that comes rarely on solace night.

How calm the breeze is, the coldness?

of it revealing everything,

my dreams in mind started taking a flight

where you hold me tight in the wonderland of LOVE

that we see in the white light of moon inside.

To know me more you have to be my Nyctophile

I will be your Odyssey – my thoughts you can compile.

I DON'T WANT THIS NIGHT TO BE OVER

NEITHER I WANT SUN TO ARISE

In the light of day where demons usually hide,

YOU GO FAR, left me behind to linger for this time

And separation gives pain where war begins

So, I DON'T WANT THIS NIGHT TO BE OVER

NEITHER I WANT SUN TO ARISE

DEAR PEN AND PAPER

To,

Dear pen and paper

Full of surprises, when the sun rises

birds fly in the blue sky, up the high.

Even the tree rejoices making rustling noise

making my beautiful surrounding with

A diverse flower on the ground.

They cheer me long,

along with me, the wind sings the song.

As I sit near beach, I found our nature

have many things to teach.

Get upside curves on my lips as

another surprise I get with the sunset.

All this I scribble becomes immortal,

breathing on this paper with

 the ink of my love and passion.

It's too hard for me to live alone

But it seems like I have found

A remedy soon.

You (pen and paper) my confiding moon,

Whether I am happy or down

You are always there to save my crown.

Something that compliments me is

PAPER and PEN.

Different shades of ink convey my emotions

To papers of my diary that have many

Untold stories behind.

Thank you for being there in my thick and thin.

Yours LOVE

Shivangi A Vivid Writer.

NOR A DISEASE NEITHER IT'S CONTAGIOUS

God has designed her with an

Extra-ordinary factor –

"A Womb" where she can bear,

A perfect place for a newborn

Replica of her.

Not a typhoon, it's just a biological cycle

that needs tampons -

A monthly companion.

Nor a disease neither it's contagious

It's a god's own gift, gives courage and

Strength makes her different.

Ohh!!!! God respect her,

She bleeds over and over again,

it keeps returning every month like rain.

She fights, makes her "knight".

She already faces mental and physical agony,

help her in 'those days' rather than making

tougher for her to survive.

Entering shrine during menorrhea is not a sin,

 don't trample her with your pricking words.

She isn't a playing doll to address your superstitions,

She is same as she is for rest of month.

Who told you a shadow of her make your pickle black?

BY THE WAY, SHE BLEEDS RED.

Don't offend me for being open,

Offended the irrational person that

is dwelling inside you.

Don't forget you are penurious of her,

She is the reason you got the

Privilege to share (The Earth).

NOT THE CAUSE OF RAPE

It's a God creation

He as Adam,

She as eve.

She has revealing

cleavage or not,

the lust inside him will

be ready to eat.

If she is slim,

She is a barbeque.

If she is fat,

She is a chicken

He lingers to taste.

If she wears BURKHA

from that black, he

figure her size and giggle her at.

If she wears white transparent top

with the colorful brazier, he

didn't get a take a time to get ERECT.

He jerks of umpteen

And if she her off,

she became an escort.

Clothes don't justify the cause of molestation or rape.

She is adult enough to make her choice;

You are no one to comment on her style.

She will wear what she like,

Doesn't need anyone suggestion to describe,

You are no one to describe.

MY MOTHERHOOD

Was a seed

Sow in a womb of a mother

Started to grow as an embryo,

Parents were unaware, as it

Was just a part of their regular night chore?

By mistake, I was broken into the

The vagina of a pure lady.

After couple of months

She felt something inside

But didn't dare to react.

Time was unstoppable,

Bump was unhide-able,

The monster suspected;

Asked the queen, in her low voice

She told the truth of conceiving.

His anger was on high,

He couldn't tolerate

And started to beat.

This time she raised her voice,

I'm not a puppet of yours.

For you, it can be a sin,

For me, it's a blessing.

I'm not a penurious of your penis

Neither of your penny.

I'm blessed I'm a lady,

Can bear a baby.

If it's not you than I have

My own place to

Live and cherish motherhood.

HAPPIEST MAN

Happiest man doesn't

Needs penny to be

In his pants,

He is already full of joy

He enjoys

And infect others too with same,

Gave wide smiles.

He is a one who makes

Others gloomy world to glitter more,

He is a man of joy

Spreads happiness Amongst all.

(Published in IN SEARCH OF HAPPINESS – an incredibly poignant piece (KDP))

MY SOUL ALREADY DIED

Bare land unable to sow,

My bae was angry, children were raw.

Dying because of drought,

 I was crushed all out.

Oh! god hell

To call self-used alcohol,

Life was tag of war,

Palms were sweating,

Rope was slipping,

I pushed my limits to heights,'

But failed at every sight.

As lands dry, my

Tears were dried up,

Performing cremation

 rituals

My soul already died.

But to repay their

Deaths, I again searched happiness,

Hope was found in the temple

Near ground, newborn was in my palms,

I nurtured as my own,

At least being a neighbor of my wife a

Children, in hell

I will not be ashamed. (Published in IN SEARCH OF HAPPINESS – an incredibly poignant piece (KDP))

FOUND MY HAPPINESS

After dine,

I was crying

Dancing with my own thoughts

Weaving some more plots,

After my breakup

I found my new crush

It was my ink, with paper white.

Serenity evolves and I rejoiced.

I was assailed and

drenched in sadness,

but I didn't lose hope and found my

happiness.

(Published in IN SEARCH OF HAPPINESS – an incredibly poignant piece (KDP))

DIVINE

It's not when man and woman lie on white bed

Their lips locked to taste and smooch like a wild

Or make out with a moan at high,

It's not when they walk long holding hand in hand,

Go for long drive with romance in the car

Or the dance in rain but still thirsty

It's not when they shop together

Or take selfies with lots of filters

It's not the HAPPINESS they are searching

It's just for the time being.

HAPPINESS is to go far away from chaos and noise,

To chase the hidden one

That can be felt when you are apart,

Just it needs the connection of soul to

Breath together the purity all,

Rest is divine to be in a relationship that shines like a gold sand flowing

In brook.

Or red lotus blossom to cherish and tucked in a hook

HAPPINESS is a smile that appears in solace or in crowed,

It's the Purity of bond that is serendipity DIVINE.

"ITS DIVINE TO HAVE A BOND THAT SHINES

It's NOT JUST A HANGOVER OF WINE"

(Published in IN SEARCH OF HAPPINESS – an incredibly poignant piece (KDP))

UNTOLD STORY

Untold, unsung, anonymous

I became a story

that you never tried to hear

I too became a story that

tried to know do you love

I bloomed in red (in love)

I went wet (in tears)

In the echoes of stories

which you never cared to read

I finally met a line that was drawn

neither black nor white

it was gray revealing the height.

(height of ignorance)

2 AM FRIEND

Think twice before uttering

a word like goodbye

there is nothing good in

adieu bye, Now its

on you 2 am friends are rare

and I have found you.

You are my somebody

To whom I can sit with

I can giggle about shits

I can talk about world

I can share my dreams which

 will never come real.

To whom I can trust blind

To whom I fight day and night

After fight, I block you from every

Possible connecting medias

But knowingly didn't block you from fon

And then a single text of you made me smile.

You are not my lover neither my bae

You are far different from these,

you are someone to whom I can relay.

My virtual 2 AM mate a genuine person

Friends without benefit

DEATH OF A RELATIONSHIP

When I got into a relationship

I thought it will be a different space

but unknowingly I invited

Chaos to come in any way.

I have many reasons to say

 this As now I have given up

and broken into many pieces.

I was cracked within,

Yelled and cried,

He enjoyed.

I was dejected

Not once but twice,

He rejoiced.

This was the

 death of a relationship

That I have buried inside.

Scattered Rays | *Shivangi Rawat*

IF AUTUMN WAS A PERSON

I miss the whiff of your scent,

I miss the long time that I have spent.

Looking at early sun and late-night moon,

I imagine your eyes melting in my heart a soon.

I wish you to know if autumn was a person

Surely it would have been you.

With silky hair and musty hands,

Resembling dried leaves, holding tree

With the last strand, before the life fall

I dream to be felt again and again

My eyes don't see you and so

I wish you to know if autumn was a person

Surely it would have been you.

I miss the amber skin flushed with the touch of our body

I feel you in here deep inside me so believe me when I say

I wish you to know if autumn was a person

Surely it would have been you.

HAVE YOU

Have you ever sunk in so deep

And chose not to return?

Have you ever allowed darkness to consume you

And sunshine to hold you for long or less?

Have you ever seen sunlight and want it

again and again to make you shine?

have you ever felt Darkness and have you

drunkenly drowned in it?

Have you ?????

CUPID HEART

After a fight, you come to me

with a chocolate and made me

to bite, wiping my tears, tucking

my hairs, you whispered in my ears

'Can be share'.

Your words were enough to melt

my heart, that day was the day we

friend zoned again and embarked.

for you, I became your best friend

silently you swept into my heart,

in this trending era, I made you my

'Password'.

I stood by you in every thick and thin,

from infant we grew matured and

so the feelings.

I lived in the "dream world of mine"

in solace, where you were my star

that shines more and more as.

Hold my hand, hugging me tight'
sudden peaks on my cheeks and
sharing bite.
All this of you I admire in nights,
Dreams and write.
Dreams of our twilight saga
where I use to visit the world that
never existed in real.
You didn't had a clue,
What chaos I was going through,
Hopes were high, I acted little shy.
As valentine day came near, I
Felted fear.
Your gesture made me believe that
You feel same as I do, indeed,
Shattering all my dreams,
You chose straight over curls,
Fashionable lenses over spectacles,
Red luscious lips over pretty smile,
Bold over fragile,

Party freak over bibliophile.

You chose physical attraction over mental connection,

You chose expensive over ordinary,

You chose seductive mind over soul

Getting cupid and nothing more.

I thought you as my Trump card

And you just Trampled my heart.

I loved you from year and

You left me in tears.

EACH TO EACH

He is in my bed

his face is a bright

light as sun rays.

I run my fingers

through his hairs,

silently he smiles,

I can feel his breath,

whispering in my ears;

All the words that I couldn't tell him

he knows it all since the start.

The beat of his heart is like

the electric current running in the wire.

My zesty symphony,

I stare transfixed, the beauty he gleams,

in this moment, I live forever

Cradled in musing.

His eyes fortified by those eyelids

how beautiful a picture it etches beneath!

He leaves me in aww with his in carnadine lips

Still pale and warm, redemption I seek.

As he dreams on, I dared to reach for the piece of heaven,

And burying my lips on his neck, I find bliss, a piece of solace,

Incentive for the battles I keep and our heart continues

Beating EACH TO EACH!

ALL I AM ASKING

All I am asking is for a moment,

All I am seeking is for a moment,

For you to turn back and see in my eyes,

For you to gaze at the devastation

That you have bought in my salvation

That you are hurriedly walking away from.

Leave behind your facades,

Leave behind your lie filled bags,

Just turn behind and see in my eyes once,

Let your eyes do the talking that has done promise of trusts.

Don't mumble lies

Don't mumble excuses

Just talk from me with your gaze.

I am waiting to welcome you,

I am waiting to travel with you

the haziest paths, the liveliest paths.

Till now I want to wipe all the gloomy moments

But, come with a firm mind,

Come with pure heart, make a promise

That now we won't live apart.

IN YOUR EMBRACE

For a moment, hold my hand tight

we are going to explore 'another' world of mine,

where we could cuddle with no hurdle,

a world where no one else other than us,

a world full of nature and fireflies,

a world where I can scream as loud as

I can "I LOVE YOU",

a world where I can lay near your heart

and hear your heartbeat without fear,

a world where I can sleep firmly in your arms

and wish for us to be together,

a world where "Nothing" last but,

want "Forever" to exist.

a world in your Embrace.

A world far from chaos, a world of dream

Without any grief.

EMBARKED ON HISTORY

The wind is blowing opposite my way

No matters what comes to me

I am going to move ahead

In this gloomy night

I will wait for the sun to rise.

Even the sky is getting darker

But that's when the star are at their

Best and so will I.

You see only the beautiful rainbow

But that too is after effect of

Sun and rain in the sky.

My courage will let it soon,

Change in my favor again.

I am alone in this hardship,

I choose odds, I want to lose

And then I will make a gateway

Through that mountain of mystery

And have my name embarked on

HISTORY.

I CRY AND BURST

There are many who shed tears in pain,

I drink them on my curvy lips.

There are many who fall and faint in heaviness of heart,

I hide them in my poems with my word.

I don't cry, I don't cry

I smile and pen-down like an

Intoxicated possessed a spirit.

By inducing them in my ink,

I give them a potion of sleep.

In my smile and word

I cry and burst.

SHHHHH ZOMBIE OR GHOST

She felt a huffle on her face,

wind of winter like a kiss of death.

As if someone on a once

Passed through her body sand congeal.

She can move a step, nor even let

Out a scream, she wishes it was a dream.

 Sudden it vanished into thin air,

In her life, she was never scared.

Seeing a loved one so long gone,

Manifest before her eyes.

As if it were still alive.

Ssshhh zombie or ghost

I'm still shocked.

ONCE IT WAS A GLORY BUT NOW IT'S A GRIEF

We killed our love as soon it begun

We are not meant to be we both said once.

We parted our ways,

You went east, I went west,

Years have passed and we aren't back.

A school reunion in GGIS,

As I entered the assembly ground,

I found you sitting beside me,

You looked at me, I looked at you and

Our heart smiled.

I never thought we will see each other again,

You are still handsome as if you didn't age

And all over again I felt my heart starts to fall.

Looking into your eyes, I just want to cry,

Remembering that day, a few years ago,

How I let you go.

For that one stupid reason, we call it Ego.

Now you are moved on with your girlfriend

And she is beautiful indeed.

My regrets are telling me that it should have been me

But I guess it was too late, so I decided to walk away

With tears in my eyes.

I will never forget this day

As for the second time, I let my love slipped away.

Maybe we are in truth not meant to be together.

FIGHT AGAINST MY ODDS

Still with blurry vision with fogginess

Searching for my unanswered questions.

I am so tired and weary,

Seeking for clarity.

I am lost running out of fuel

It is getting dark and so cold.

'I am trying to explore the

Depths of the unknown me.

Finding 'me' to move on from

The turmoil I am phasing.

I am scared of this havoc in my mind,

But I am determined.

Determined to be strong and

Fight back all the ODDs.

ORCHESTRA

Lub Dub Lub Dub of your heart

Is a pleasant music for my ears.

It is a melody of soul,

It is a sign of life,

It reminds me of hope.

A song in a minor key,

Hearts beat Lub-Dub in perfect harmony.

Yours and my heartbeats together

form an ORCHESTRA for a perfect

Love ceremony.

IT WAS TULIP, ROSE, AND DAFFODILS

Sitting on the grass, admiring the grace

It was Tulip, Rose, and Daffodils

dancing with the waves of wind.

I was an audience watching them on stage, as if.

They brought peace to my heart,

made me calm and showed the

direction for my lost soul.

They made me realize how

brave I am, to still be here

after a violent storm that

took an hour ago.

Scattered Rays | *Shivangi Rawat*

MY FATHER

To raise a girl child

It's hard for a little while,

But,

My father has set a bar high

And made all the women stay aside

He made me stand

He made me talk

He made me walk

He is my pillar of strength,

Sacrificing his youth, he nurtured

He taught, to be a girl with a spine

Never to give up in breakdowns,

He taught me the meaning of laugh,

Not to shed tears, be as strong as tor

And go to war,

Yes, I am a proud daughter of yours.

You are My father,

Scattered Rays | *Shivangi Rawat*

You are my friend

You will only there for me

till the end.

THEY MADE ME MURDERER

A girl born from my womb

has died a premature death,

I carry her cold body on

My aching shoulders,

Seeking a place to

Burry her,

Being a mother,

eyes full of tears

I tried to weave a shroud

Out of my wounded heart

But each time I sew it

There left a gaping hole

Like the Gulf of sin

Trying to suck me into it.

(Ache of a woman who killed a girl child, society behind the sin)

MY DREAM

I slipped under the quilt

beneath the pillow's spell,

I softly drift into heaven from hell.

A journey I was carving

A journey that fills my being

My lips were smiling

The blind girl now becomes the seeing one

The lonely lady now becomes the lover

And the childless woman now becomes the caring mother.

 Reflection of my dormant fear

I was woken and broken into tears.

IT WAS A DREAM!

With sleep, I am free to prey

On untold thoughts which nightly stray.

TO BE HIS WIFE

He; a drop of rain on a hot summer sand.

He; the beat of my heart and the air of my lungs breath.

He; the sun, the moon, the wind and the autumn's golden leaves.

He; is the warm feeling I get, when I remember him tucking me in solace.

He; being the world's best entrepreneur, treats me like queen becomes my pawn.

He; makes me laugh with his silly tongue

He; is the mixed emotions (of mine)

He; is the scared feeling I have when he comes late

Being tired and stressed he smiles,

His beautiful smile becomes light in the darkest night.

I always cherish the wonderful time we have spent.

The best part of my life is to be his wife.

ANGEL

I ponder sometimes

where you hide your wings

Are they hung in your closet?

with the rest of your things???

Do you keep them away, and

use them during chaos and peace,

or you give them to polish, so they

can be wide and bright.

I know you have two wings,

Where your two daughters swing.

It's true

"GOD always gives them to Angel like you"

My dear dad

We love you; you are our strength and pride

We are blessed to have ANGEL in life like you.

A WISH....

…. and my eyes espy Hesper,

Twilight and vibes are felt

you are by my side….

Every night I want

to hug you tight,

immersed in deep

search of my asylum

in your lap for a

warm and safe nap.

Dear Maa,

I will meet you again in the stars...

Will form a constellation,

a glittery dime will set on fire.

(Dream of a daughter without mother

Why she left her in others hand?

Why daughter was not blessed to be nurtured by her?

www.ingramcontent.com/pod-product-compliance
Lightning Source LLC
Chambersburg PA
CBHW032005060426
42449CB00031B/517